THE WINTER CHOCOLATE BAKEBOOK

Stephanie Laurent

PREFACE OF THE PUBLISHER

We are pleased that you have chosen this book. If you are in possession of a paperback book, we will gladly send you the same as an e-book, then you can easily turn the pages digitally as well as normally.

We attach great importance to the fact that all of our authors, when creating their own cookbooks, have recooked all of their recipes several times.
Therefore, the quality of the design of the recipes and the instructions for recooking are detailed and will certainly succeed.

Our authors strive to optimize your recipes, but tastes are and will always be different!

We at Mindful Publishing support the creation of the books, so that the creative authors of the recipes can take their time and enjoy cooking.

We appreciate your opinion about our recipes, so we would appreciate your review of the book and your experience with these great recipes!

In order to reduce the printing costs of our books and to offer the possibility to offer recipes in books at all, we have to do without pictures in the cookbooks. The digital version has the same content as the paperback.

Our recipes will convince you and reveal to you

a culinary style you can't get enough of!

Enough of the foreword, let the recipes begin!

CHOCOLATE CAKE WITH ORANGE FLAVOURING

Average level

Ingredients

1 orange
100g pastry chocolate
3 eggs
280g of sugar
240ml sunflower oil
25g cocoa powder (unsweetened)
250g of flour
1 teaspoon baking soda

Preparation

Wash the orange and pierce it very deeply with a pick or fork. Dip the orange in a saucepan with water. Make sure it is completely covered and cook for about 40 min. After cooking, remove the orange and let it cool slightly. Then cut it in half, remove the pits and blend it completely to obtain a fine purée. Allow to cool completely.
Melt the chocolate in a water bath.
In a bowl, mix the eggs with the sugar and oil, then gently add the orange puree and melted chocolate (which should be slightly cooled).
In another bowl, mix the flour with the cocoa powder and

baking soda and then add the orange-chocolate mixture. Mix everything well and then pour the batter into a well-buttered cake tin. Preheat the oven to 160°C (gas mark 5) and bake the cake for about 40 minutes. Make sure that the cake does not start overbaking. To check the baking, you can prick the cake in the middle with a wooden pick or toothpick. If the dough does not stick, the cake is well done. Take out of the oven and let it cool for 10 min. Remove the pan and let cool completely. Chocolate filling: Bring the liquid cream to the boil and pour it over the chocolate pastry broken into small pieces (be careful, mix in a baking bowl). Mix well - you can use a blender. Let the cream rest for at least 30 minutes to get a better consistency. Then garnish the tart on top and sides. You can decorate the cake with the slices of fine almonds. Let the cake rest for several hours in the refrigerator. It is even better the next day....

ROYAL WALNUT CAKE

very easy

Ingredients

1 packet of spoon cookies
1 glass of kirsch
250g of butter
2 eggs
200g of sugar
125g almond powder
125g of walnut powder
Whipped cream for the decor
Candied fruit for decoration

Preparation

Mix the butter in ointment with the sugar.
Add the egg yolks, almonds and walnuts. Mix everything together. Add the egg whites beaten into snow.
Place a greaseproof paper in a cake tin. Place a layer of spoon cookies soaked in a mixture of kirsch and cold water.
Place a layer of the nut mixture on top.
Alternate layers of cookie mixture until the cake tin is completely filled and finish with cookies.
Put a baking paper and a weight on the cake and place in the fridge for 24 hours.
Unmould and decorate with cream and candied fruit.

PAVEMENT OF SMALL CHOCOLATE BUTTERS WITHOUT COOKING

very easy

Ingredients

1 packet of small buttered cakes and cookies
1 box of chocolate dessert cream type Mont Blanc or Danette
1 lait

Preparation

Dip the small butters in the milk.
Place the cookies side by side in a dish.
Alternate layers of chocolate cream and small butters.
At the end, cover the whole with a good
layer of Mont Blanc chocolate.
and put in the fridge for 30 minutes.
To your little spoons!

YOGHURT AND APPLE CAKE WITH CHOCOLATE ICING

easy

Ingredients

1 packet of baking powder
1 pot of plain yogurt
1/2 jar of oil
2 jars of sugar
3 pots of flour
3 eggs
2 apples
1/2 plate of chocolate nestlé dessert for icing

Preparation

Preheat your oven to 180°C (thermostat 6).
Mix all ingredients in order.
Cut the apples into the thinnest possible slices.
Add the apples to the dough and mix.
Butter a cake tin and pour the dough into it.
Put in the oven for about 30 minutes at 180°C (thermostat 6).
For glazing:
Melt the 1/2 plate of chocolate in a bain marie and coat the cake with it.
Wait for the cake to cool before serving.

CARIBBEAN BANANA AND CHOCOLATE CAKE

very easy

Ingredients

1 puff pastry
200g of chocolate
6 eggs
2 bananas
Grated coconut

Preparation

Spread the puff pastry on a baking sheet and prick it with a fork. Bake in the oven for about 10 minutes, making sure it does not swell.
Prepare the chocolate mousse.
When the pastry is cooked, let it cool, then spread the chocolate mousse over it, cut banana slices and place them on top of the mousse. Sprinkle with grated coconut and put in the fridge.

SUPER EASY CHOCOLATE PUFF PASTRY CAKE

very easy

Ingredients

1 puff pastry (ready-made)
2 chocolate bars (about 360 g)

Preparation

Preheat your oven to 200°C (thermostat 6-7).
Roll out the puff pastry on your baking sheet.
Place the chocolate bars inside over half of the puff pastry.
Fold the puff pastry in half, turning over
the edges to close the cake.
Put in the oven for about 20 to 30 minutes, keeping
an eye on the dough for crispness.

CHOCOLATE CHIP SWISS PAVING STONE

easy

Ingredients

1 rectangular puff pastry
40cl of milk
1 egg
50g of sugar
50g of flour
2 sachets of vanilla sugar
150g of chocolate

Preparation

Boil the milk with a sachet of vanilla sugar in a saucepan.
Mix the egg, sugar and the second sachet of vanilla sugar in a bowl.
Stir in flour and milk.
Put the whole on the heat and bring to the boil. Reserve the pastry cream obtained.
Spread the puff pastry on the worktop and put pastry cream on half of the dough.
Spread the chocolate chips on the pastry cream.
Close the puff pastry half on the part covered with ingredients.
Cut the puff pastry into slices (will form the size of your Swiss pavés), then place on a baking tray covered with baking paper.
Bake for 15 minutes at 210°C (gas mark 7).

FONDANT WHITE CHOCOLATE, COCONUT, RASPBERRIES

easy

Ingredients

1 shortbread paste
250g of mascarpone
100g of sugar
100g of coconut
100g of white chocolate
2 eggs
100g of fresh or frozen raspberries

Preparation

Mix the mascarpone, sugar, coconut and eggs.
Grate the white chocolate and incorporate it into the preparation.
Spread the dough in small moulds (tartlet type).
Put the raspberries at the bottom of the mould and the preparation on top.
Put in a hot oven at 200°C (th.6/7) for about 20 minutes.

MUFFINS WITH LIGHT CHOCOLATE FONDANT HEART (WITHOUT BUTTER)

very easy

Ingredients

1 small jar of compote (95gr) I put some pear compote without added sugar.
150g of dark chocolate pastry
3 egg trails
20g of flour
20g of cornstarch
10g of sugar (optional, the sugar compote already)

Preparation

- heat the oven to 240 degrees (th8).
- melt the chocolate in the microwave with a little water (40 seconds) stir and put the compote, put back 30 seconds. Mix well.
- Mix the eggs, flour and cornstarch. Incorporate the melted chocolate, mix to obtain a very smooth preparation.
- Put the whole in small silicone moulds.
Put in the oven for 4 minutes to obtain a flowing heart. (5 minutes for large muffins).
PS: for those who like it sweeter, you can put 10gr of sugar

(a tablespoon) but the sugar compote still a little.

SOFT CAKE WITH CHESTNUTS, CHOCOLATE AND RUM

very easy

Ingredients

1 small jar of chestnut cream
100g of chocolate
80g of butter 80g of flour 1 soupspoon of rum, 3 yolks and 4 egg whites

Preparation

Melt the chocolate and butter Add the 3 yolks, the chestnut cream, the flour and the rum, mix, whisk the whites into snow and delicately mix the whole, butter and flour a mould and cook at 190 c 15min then lower the temperature to 175c for 15min.

VERY CHOCOLATE FONDANT WITH MATCHA TEA

very easy

Ingredients

1 small box of matcha tea
200g of dark chocolate
150g of butter
50g brown sugar
50g of flour
100g of liquid fresh cream
3 eggs

Preparation

Preheat the oven to 150°C (thermostat 5).
Melt the chocolate with the butter in a bain-marie.
In a bowl, mix the eggs, sugar, cream and flour.
Add the melted chocolate to the preparation. Mix well.
Butter a brownie mould and pour the preparation into it.
Cook for 10 minutes.
At the exit of the oven, sprinkle with Matcha tea everywhere (in rather fine layer however). Wait for the cake to cool down before tasting…

DARK CHOCOLATE, CHERRY AND HAZELNUT BROWNIES

easy

Ingredients

1 handful of red cherries
60g of flour
100g of dark chocolate
125g of buttered butter
175g brown sugar
50g of hazelnuts
2 eggs
1/2 teaspoon vanilla powder
1 tablespoon almond powder
25g of cerealecountry crips (optional)

Preparation

Preheat the oven to thermostat 6 (180 °C), melt the chocolate and butter.
Beat the eggs, sugar and vanilla powder in a bowl.
Add the chocolate, almond powder, flour and hazelnuts. Add the pitted cherries (the equivalent of a full bowl) to the mixture.
Pour into a buttered mould, put in the oven for 30 minutes, checking regularly by pricking with a toothpick, as soon as it comes out intact, it's ready!

CHOCOLATE MOELLEUX, PEAR AND PEPPER

easy

Ingredients

1 Comice pear
4 eggs
125g dark chocolate for dessert
85g powdered sugar
65g of butter
25g of flour
Pepper from the mill

Preparation

Preheat the furnace to 200°C (thermostat 6-7).
Peel and dice the pear.
Butter 4 individual moulds.
Separate the whites from the yolks and beat them until stiff.
Put the chocolate in a water bath and add the caster sugar.
Once the chocolate has melted, add the egg yolks,
butter, pepper and flour off the heat.
Whip the mixture until it becomes smooth, then add the pear cubes. Gently stir in the egg whites with a wooden spoon.
Pour the dough into the moulds and bake in the oven for 8 minutes. Turn out of the moulds and serve hot.

CHOCOLATE RASPBERRY FONDANT

very easy

Ingredients

1 jar of raspberry jam
230g of chocolate
2 tablespoons of coffee
80g of butter
3 tablespoons of fresh cream
4 eggs
30g of flour + a pinch of salt
30g of cornstarch
1 sachet of baking powder
50g of almond slivers

Preparation

Preheat the oven to 200°C (thermostat 6-7).
Melt the chocolate with the coffee and butter.
Beat the jam with the eggs with a whisk for 3 min, add the fresh cream, then the sifted flours and the yeast. Mix well and add the melted chocolate while stirring with a wooden spoon. Fill the mini moulds to 3/4, sprinkle with slivered almonds. Bake for 15 to 18 minutes in the oven at 180°C (thermostat 6), rotating heat.

YOGHURT-NECTARINE-CHOCOLATE CHIP CAKE

easy

Ingredients

1 pot of yoghurt
1 jar of yoghurt and oil
2 eggs
200g of sugar
250g of flour
1 sachet of yeast
1 sachet of vanilla sugar
2 nectarines
100g of chocolate

Preparation

Preheat the oven to 180°C (thermostat 6).
Peel and cut the nectarines into small pieces.
Mix the eggs, sugar and vanilla sugar.
Add the yoghurt and then the oil - mix well.
Stir in the flour and baking powder.
Finally add the chocolate chips and nectarines.
Butter and flour a mould and pour the mixture into it.
Bake in the oven for 35 minutes, keeping an eye on the end of the baking time.

BLACK FOREST CUTS

easy

Ingredients

1 pot of yoghurt
2 jars of sugar
3 pots of flour
1/2 bag of baking powder
3 eggs
1/2 jar of melted butter
200g of pastry chocolate
1 jar of cherry jam (or raspberry jam)
1 whipped cream

Preparation

Preheat the oven at thermostat 6-7 (200°C).
In a bowl, mix the yoghurt, sugar, flour and baking powder. Add the eggs and mix again, then add the chocolate and melted butter.
Butter a mould and flour it. Pour the dough into the mould and bake for 30 min.
Once the cake is cooked, cut it into small squares and let it cool.
Once the chocolate cake cubes have cooled, arrange them in 8 to 10 cups (e.g. glasses or stemmed glasses):
- a layer of chocolate cake cubes
- a layer of jam
- a layer of chocolate cake cubes
- a layer of whipped cream

YOGHURT, HAZELNUT AND CHOCOLATE CHIP CAKE

easy

Ingredients

1 pot of yoghurt
2 jars of powdered sugar
3 pots of flour
1/2 jar of oil
3 eggs
1 sachet of baking powder
200g of shelled hazelnuts
100g of special dessert chocolates or chocolate chips
Butter for the mould

Preparation

Preheat the oven to 150°C (thermostat 5).
Pour the contents of the yoghurt pot into a salad bowl.
Keep the empty yoghurt pot for measuring purposes.
Add all the other ingredients up to the hazelnuts,
mix well with a mixer.
Keep some hazelnuts whole.
Coarsely grind the rest of the hazelnuts as well as the 1/2
chocolate plate and keep a few chocolate chips.
Add to the previous mixture.
Butter a cake tin and fill it with the yoghurt mixture.

Sprinkle the top with the whole hazelnuts
and the preserved chocolate chips.
Bake the cake for 45 minutes.
Check the baking time by dipping a knife blade into the cake.

YOGHURT, PEAR AND CHOCOLATE CAKE

easy

Ingredients

1 pot of yoghurt
2 jars of caster sugar
1 sachet of baking powder
3 pots of flour
1 jar of chocolate noodles
3/4 jar of oil
3 eggs
3 pears

Preparation

Heat the oven at thermostat 6 (180°C).
Peel and seed the pears, then cut them in half
and then into small slices. Keep.
Put the yoghurt in a shallow dish, then wash the jar
in order to use it for the other ingredients.
Mix the yoghurt, sugar, and whole eggs
until it becomes a little foamy.
Add the flour and baking powder. Stir to combine.
Then add the oil little by little until the mixture
is smooth and even.
Then gradually stir in the pear pieces, stirring gently
and add the chocolate vermicelli, stirring again.
Butter or oil a cake tin.

Pour the mixture over the entire surface and
then add the few reserved pear pieces.
Bake for 45 minutes at half height.
The cake is cooked when you push in a knife
and the tip comes out dry.
Enjoy cold or warm.

LIGHT BANANA, TRUFFLE CHOCOLATE AND WALNUT CAKE

easy

Ingredients

1 pot of yoghurt
2 jars of yoghurt) brown sugar or brown sugar (or 1 jar of whole sugar)
3 jars of flour (possibly a little more if too liquid)
2 egg trails
1/2 jar of peanut or sunflower oil
1 mashed and pureed banana
10 coarsely chopped walnuts (which can be lightly toasted in a frying pan)
Rhumambré
100g of chocolate melted in a bain-marie in a little milk (you can include 40g of spice chocolate)
Cinnamon (except if using spice chocolate)
1 sachet of yeast
Orangemoyenne (you can add its zest if it is not treated)
1 pinch of salt
Powdered sugar

Preparation

For the material, think of 1 salad bowl, 1 manual whisk (much better than the fork, 1 thrifty knife if necessary).

Preheat the oven to 160°C (thermostat 5/6).
Put the chocolate to melt gently in a bain-marie in a little milk.
In the meantime, empty the yoghurt pot
into the salad bowl and rinse it.
With the hand whisk, mix the yoghurt with the
sugar and then add the flour and salt.
Add the eggs, oil, rum, orange juice (and its zest if not processed), cinnamon (unless the chocolate is already spicy), crushed banana, chopped (possibly roasted) nuts and truffle chocolate and mix (possibly add up to 1/2 pot of flour if it is too liquid).
Add yeast and mix for 1 minute.
Prepare the mould: put baking paper in the bottom
of the mould and pour the machine into it.
Put in the oven and bake at gas mark 6/7 for about
1 hour (make sure to cover it so that it does not
burn) without opening the oven door.
When the cake is cooked (the blade of the knife
must come out dry), let it cool on a rack.
You can sprinkle with powdered sugar.

CHOCOLATE CAKE FOR AND BY CHILDREN

very easy

Ingredients

1 pot of yoghurt
3 pots of flour
2 jars of sugar
2 jars of chocolate powder
1 jar of oil
3 eggs
1 sachet of yeast

Preparation

Start by putting the contents of the yogurt in your blender. Then wash, rinse and dry the jar, it will serve as a measure.
Add the flour, eggs and mix.
Add the sugar and the chocolate powder; mix.
Add the yeast, and save the jar of oil for the end (so you don't have a sticky jar for the rest of the ingredients!).
Mix long enough; the more you mix, the softer the cake will be.
Butter and flour your pan, then pour the batter into it.
Bake for 30 minutes at 200°C (gas mark 6-7), on convection heat. Keep an eye on the cake and only take it out when the blade of your knife is dry.
If you want to make an icing on top, melt dark chocolate in a saucepan, add 1 teaspoon of butter and 4 tablespoons of powdered sugar. Spread on the unmoulded

cake and let it dry; it's crunchy!

YOGHURT, PEAR, ALMOND, PECAN AND CHOCOLATE CAKE

Average level

Ingredients

1 jar of pear flavoured yoghurt
3 eggs
1 jar of sugar
3 pots of flour T45
1 sachet of baking powder
1/2 jar of oil
125g of almond slivers
3 pears (small)

Preparation

The sponge cake :
Preheat the oven to 180°C (thermostat 6).
Prepare the dough:
Mix 3 whole eggs, yoghurt, sugar, flour, yeast and oil.
Peel, seed and dice the pears. Fry them in a frying pan in a little butter. Add the cooled pear cubes to the dough.
Toast the slivered almonds in the pan. Add them to the dough.
Pour the preparation into a buttered pan.
Bake in the oven for 40 min.
When the dough is cooked, let it cool on a wire rack, then cut it in half lengthwise.

The pear cream:
Mix 2 pears (peeled and deseeded) with 20 cl of liquid crème fraiche and 1 tablespoon of sugar.
Dissolve 1 tablespoon of maïzéna in the milk.
Mix in a saucepan the mixed pears and the diluted maïzéna.
Heat over low heat, stirring until the mixture thickens.
The icing:
Melt 200 g of dark chocolate with 1 tablespoon of water in the microwave or in a bain marie. Obtain a smooth mixture.
Mix the melted chocolate with 2 tablespoons of powdered sugar.
Assemble the cake:
Spread the pear cream on the half cake.
Arrange the second half of the cake.
Spread the chocolate icing with a spatula on top.
Arrange some pecans and pear slices on top of the cake.

LIGHT CHOCOLATE CAKE WITH ORANGE CHIPS

very easy

Ingredients

1 jar of stirred yogurt
2 jars of flour
2 jars of sugar
1 jar of cornstarch
1/2 packet of yeast
4 tablespoons of milk
1/3 jar of oil
200g of chocolate with orange pieces
3 eggs

Preparation

Melt the chocolate with a little water.
Add the eggs, sugar, milk then flour, cornstarch, yeast and oil.
Mix until you obtain a fluid and homogeneous dough.
Butter your mould to be missed and put in the oven
at 200°C (thermostat 7) for 35 minutes.
Monitor the baking process regularly.

YOGHURT CAKE, SPECULOOS AND CHOCOLATE CHIPS

very easy

Ingredients

1 pot of plain yogurt
1 jar of yoghurt and oil
3 jars of speculoos yoghurt mixed in small pieces
1/2 jar of sugar yoghurt
1 sachet of baking powder
150g of dark chocolate
4 eggs

Preparation

Preheat the oven to 180°C (thermostat 6).
Mix the yoghurt, powdered speculoos, egg
yolks, sugar, yeast and oil.
Beat the egg whites until stiff and fold
them gently into the mixture.
Break the chocolate so as to obtain more or less large chips.
Add the chips to the mixture.
Pour the preparation into a buttered mould
and put in the oven for 45 minutes.
Turn out of the mould, eat warm, the chocolate is still melted....

YOGHURT AND CHOCOLATE COFFEE CAKE

very easy

Ingredients

1 pot of plain yogurt
2 jars of sugar
1 pot of flour
1 jar of corn flour or cornflour
1 pot of almond powder
75g of butter + 10 g for the mould
100g of dark chocolate
2 spoonfuls of very strong ground coffee
1 sachet of yeast and vanilla sugar
4 eggs
Grated coconut

Preparation

Put the yoghurt pot in a bowl and clean it.
Take the pot and measure the flours and sieve them together in a bowl, then add the sugar, yeast, vanilla sugar and the two teaspoons.
Melt the chocolate in the microwave with the butter for about 1 min or more depending on the power.
In the salad bowl, add the whole, the contents of the natural yoghurt pot, the eggs, the chocolate so that the mixture is homoge-

neous and put it in the oven for 40 min at 180°C (thermostat 6).

CHOCOLATE-BANANA YOGHURT CAKE

very easy

Ingredients

1 pot of plain yogurt (100 g)
2 jars of sugar
3 pots of flour
1/2 jar of oil
2 eggs
1/2 bag of baking powder
1 sachet of vanilla sugar
1 g of dark chocolate
1 teaspoon of honey
1 banana

Preparation

Preheat the oven to 150°C (thermostat 5).
Melt the chocolate in a water bath.
Mix the plain yoghurt with the sugar and vanilla sugar.
Add the 2 eggs, the flour and the oil, mix and put
the melted chocolate in the preparation and add
the baking powder at the last moment.
Cut the banana into slices, put half of it in the bottom of a cake
tin, preferably non-stick, and pour half of the preparation,
add the rest of the banana and the rest of the preparation.
You can draw the shape you want on the cake with
honey before baking, success guaranteed.

CHOCOLATE VANILLA YOGHURT CAKE

very easy

Ingredients

1 pot of yoghurt (the pot is then used as a measure)
1.5 pot of yoghurt flour
1.5 pot of corn yogurt
2 eggs
1 sachet of vanilla sugar
1 sachet of baking powder
1/2 jar of yoghurt and oil
200g of dark pastry chocolate
1 teaspoon of liquid vanilla flavouring (optional)

Preparation

Preheat your oven to 200°C, thermostat 6/7, and butter your mould.
In a bowl, mix the eggs, sugars, yoghurt, flour, cornstarch and yeast.
Using an electric mixer, beat the ingredients until you obtain a smooth dough.
Melt the chocolate in a water bath for 5 minutes.
Add the chocolate to the dough and mix.
Add the oil and the liquid vanilla flavouring.
Pour the dough into a mould and bake your cake for 25 minutes.

COFFEE-CHOCOLATE FONDANT

very easy

Ingredients

1 pot of coffee yoghurt
200g of dark chocolate
60g of flour
60g of hazelnut powder
3 eggs
60g of sugar
1 tablespoon coffee powder
1 tablespoon cocoa powder

Preparation

Preheat the oven to 250°C (th 8-9).
To make bleach eggs and sugar.
Sieve together the flour and the powder of hazelnuts.
Melt the chocolate in a bain-marie.
Mix the yoghurt, the flour, the hazelnut powder, the eggs, the sugar, the coffee powder and finally the cocoa.
Add the melted chocolate and smooth.
Bake for 20 min at 200°C (th 6-7), let cool and unmould.

CHOCOLATE AND PEAR YOGHURT CAKE

easy

Ingredients

1 sachet of yeast
1 pot of yoghurt and pear
1/2 jar of oil (= 10cl)
1.5 pot of sugar (= 30cl)
1.5 pot of flour (= 30cl)
2 eggs
200g of dark chocolate

Preparation

Simply mix the ingredients one by one, in the order above.
Melt the chocolate and mix with the preparation.
Pour the batter into a cake pan.
Bake at 180°C (thermostat 6) for about 30 min.
Check the baking with the tip of a knife,
which should come out dry.

VANILLA CAKE WITH A CHOCOLATE TILE

easy

Ingredients

1 sachet of yeast
1 yurt
1/4 jar of yoghurt and olive oil
3/4 jar of yoghurt oil
2 jars of sugar yogurt
3 eggs
4 pots of yoghurt flour
3 vanilla beans
10 squares of chocolate

Preparation

Preheat the oven to 180°C (thermostat 6).
Mix the yoghurt with the sugar.
Add the baking powder to the flour.
Gradually add the flour and baking powder to the yoghurt and sugar mixture and mix.
Then remove the vanilla beans from the mixture.
Add the oil and mix.
Add your preparation in small ramekins.
Bake in the oven at 180°C (gas mark 6).
After a few minutes, look at your cakes, if they are just starting to bake, harden a little, add the chocolate squares.
Let continue baking for 15 min.

Here it is ready!

CHOCOLATE FONDANT

very easy

Ingredients

1 bar of NESTLÉ DESSERT Dark Chocolate
4 eggs
100g of butter
60g of sugar
50g of flour

Preparation

Preheat your oven to thermostat 6/7 (200°C) and melt the chocolate and butter cut into pieces in a saucepan over very low heat. In a bowl, add the sugar, eggs, flour and chocolate. Mix well. Butter and flour your mould and pour the cake dough. Bake in the oven for about 10 to 11 minutes. When the cake comes out of the oven, it does not seem to be sufficiently baked. This is normal, let it cool down and then unmould it.

CHOCOLATE EASTER NEST CAKE

easy

Ingredients

1 bar of NESTLÉ DESSERT Dark Chocolate
5 eggs
125g of butter
150g of sugar
100g of almond powder
50g of flour

Preparation

Preheat the oven to gas mark 6 (180°C), break 200 g of chocolate into small pieces and melt it in the microwave for 2 minutes at 500W. Remove from the heat, add 125 g of butter in small pieces and mix well. Break the eggs, separating the yolks from the whites, beat the yolks with the sugar and gradually add the melted chocolate and butter, flour and almond powder. Beat the egg whites until stiff with a pinch of salt and gently fold into the previous mixture. Bake this mixture in a buttered crown mould for 30 minutes in the oven, remove from the mould and leave to cool on a wire rack. For the icing, melt the chocolate broken into pieces with the water, add the butter and mix well, then gradually add the pow-

dered sugar. Pour the icing over the cake and coat it completely.
Place in the refrigerator for 1 hour.
Decorate the center of the cake with fried chocolate
and small Easter eggs.

ABSOLUTE DARK CHOCOLATE FONDANT

very easy

Ingredients

1 tablet of NESTLÉ DESSERT Dark Absolute Chocolate
50g of flour
50g of sugar
90g of butter
3 eggs

Preparation

Preheat your oven in traditional mode at thermostat 6/7 (200°C) and melt the chocolate with the butter for 1 minute 30 to 500 W. Add the eggs, sugar and flour and pour into 6 small muffin tins. Bake in the oven for 12 minutes.

CHOCOLATE FONDANT

very easy

Ingredients

1 bar of dark chocolate
100g of butter
100g of sugar

Preparation

Preheat your oven Th 6/7 (200 degrees)
Melt the chocolate and butter in pieces 2min
at 500W in the microwave.
Add the sugar, eggs, flour. Mix well.
Butter and flour your mould and pour the dough.

BAYAH BROWNIE

very easy

Ingredients

1 bar of dark chocolate (200 g)
4 eggs
100g powdered sugar
2 flour
1 pinch of salt
100g of butter
2 sachets of vanilla sugar

Preparation

Melt the chocolate with the butter.
Separate the whites and yolks.
Mix the yolks, sugar, vanilla sugar and flour.
Beat the whites until stiff and then fold in.
Cook for 5 minutes in the microwave in a transparent dish with a diameter of about 20-25 cm.

STRACCIATELLA STYLE CHOCOLATE CAKE

easy

Ingredients

1 bar of dark chocolate 170 g
100g of butter
3 eggs
20g powdered sugar
100g of flour

Preparation

Melt the butter.
In a bowl, mix the melted butter, eggs, flour and sugar.
Separate the dough obtained in two: crush three squares of chocolate and melt the rest of the chocolate, (I put my chocolate that I have broken into squares in a bowl with a lid, I pour boiling water over it and put the lid back on and after about 2 minutes I remove the water).
Mix the melted chocolate with half of the dough.
and add the three crushed chocolate squares
to the other half of the dough.
In a buttered 24 cm diameter mould, alternate
the layers of the two pastes obtained.
Bake at 210°C (th 7) for about 12 minutes.

DARK CHOCOLATE, ALMOND OR HAZELNUT PAVING STONE

easy

Ingredients

1 bar of dark chocolate for dessert
3 eggs
50g of butter
50g of flour
200g of ground almonds or hazelnuts

Preparation

Melt the chocolate in a water bath (or in the microwave with a little water).
As soon as the chocolate is melted, add the butter and mix well.
Add the eggs, one after the other, stir well (with a small whisk).
Add the flour, then finish with the ground almonds or hazelnuts, mix well.
Butter a cookie tin, pour the mixture.
Put the preparation 25 mn Th 5-6.
The success of this cake will depend on the baking time, the cake must remain soft, just cooked.
When the cake is cooled, cut small squares and arrange them

on a dish or in a cake tin...it is a delight with a good coffee.

CHOCOLATE MOELLEUX AND ST MORET

easy

Ingredients

1 bar of pastry chocolate
130g brown sugar
2 eggs
150g of Saint Morêt
30g of cocoa
100g of flour
1/2 bag of yeast
25g of soft butter

Preparation

Melt the chocolate in pieces and butter together in the microwave for 1.30 minutes and then mix.
Beat the eggs, sugar and St Moret together.
Mix these 2 preparations.
Add the flour, the yeast and the sifted cocoa.
Pour in a mould (preferably cake mould) then put in the oven for 15 min at 180°C (thermostat 6).
Keep in a cool place because the cake is eaten cold.

ALL CHOCOLATE EXTRA MELTING CAKE (WITHOUT BUTTER OR FLOUR)

easy

Ingredients

1 bar of kitchen chocolate (200 g)
100g of chocolate powder
4 eggs
1 pot of fresh cream (20 cl)
1 bottle of whipping cream
200g of powdered sugar
2 tablespoons of vanilla
1 sachet of baking powder

Preparation

Melt the chocolate bar with the fresh cream, then add the chocolate powder, the yeast sachet and the 4 egg yolks. Whisk the egg whites and add them to the previous mixture to make a mousse.
Make a whipped cream with the whipped cream, sugar and vanilla flavouring. (Tip: also add a bag of whipped cream).
Mix the two preparations.
Put in a large round buttered mould.

Bake for 1h30 at 130°C (thermostat 4-5) at half height.
Watch the baking process!
(the oven does not need to be preheated or else reduce the baking time by 1/2 hour).

BROWNIES WITHOUT BAKING

very easy

Ingredients

1 cup of finely chopped walnuts (actually the amount of walnuts depends a little on the taste of each)
80g of unsweetened chocolate
1 can of sweetened condensed milk
48 vanilla wafers that you have taken care to crumble into pieces

Preparation

Sprinkle half of the chopped walnuts on the bottom of a square pan.
In a saucepan, melt the chocolate in the sweetened condensed milk over low heat.
Cook the mixture, stirring, until it has thickened, for about 10 minutes.
Remove from the heat.
Stir in wafer crumbs and remaining chopped nuts.
Spread mixture into prepared pan.
Spread remaining chopped walnuts over mixture.
Refrigerate for 4 hours until firm.
Cut into squares.

CHOCOLATE CAKE (EASY)

easy

Ingredients

1 glass of flour
1 glass of sugar
200g of chocolate (dark or milk)
50g of butter
4 eggs

Preparation

Preheat your oven to 180°C.
Melt the chocolate and butter in a saucepan (medium size) with a little water over medium heat.
Off the heat add the sugar and mix.
Add the egg yolks and keep the whites.
Add the flour and mix.
Beat the egg whites until stiff and mix into the dough.
Pour the mixture into a buttered (and possibly floured) mould and bake for 30 minutes at 180°C.

CHOCOLATE CAKE (MILK AND GLUTEN FREE)

very easy

Ingredients

1 glass of chestnut flour
1 glass of rice milk
1 soya yogurt
3 tablespoons of cane sugar
50g of chocolate
1/2 bag of yeast without gluten
3 eggs

Preparation

Melt the chocolate in the rice milk, very slowly. Mix the chestnut flour with the baking powder and sugar. Add to this mixture the eggs, the soy yoghurt, and the chocolatey rice milk. Mix everything well. Pour into a round mold, and put in the oven for 20 minutes at 200°C (th 6-7). It is cooked, when the tip of the knife planted in the cake comes out barely moist.

SOFT COCONUT MILK AND CHOCOLATE CHIPS.

very easy

Ingredients

1 glass of coconut milk
2 glasses of flour
1 glass of sugar
1 half glass of oil
4 eggs
100g of chocolate

Preparation

Preheat the oven to 170 degrees.
Separate the egg whites from the yolks, beat the yolks with the sugar and gradually add the flour. Add oil and coconut milk.
Mix well until you obtain a smooth dough.
Add the chocolate chips.
Beat the egg whites until stiff and gently fold them into the previous mixture.
Pour the dough into a 22cm springform pan.

APRICOT MILK CAKE (CHOCOLATE MARBLED)

very easy

Ingredients

1 glass of semi-skimmed milk
2.5 glass of flour without lumps
1.5 glass of caster sugar
1/2 glass of oil
1 sachet of vanilla sugar
1 sachet of baking powder (11 g)
3 eggs - very small

Preparation

Plan:
- 1 plastic glass (= scaler)
- 1 nonstick run-out mold

Mix all the ingredients of PART A to make a homogeneous paste that is neither too liquid nor too thick.
Taste it, it is delicious for raw dough lovers....
In a cup, put PART B. Put the cup in the microwave to melt, and mix well once the mixture has melted.
Extract 2 tablespoons of the dough made at the beginning and add it to the cup, mix. It must remain dark all the same.
In your mould to be missed to put at the bottom 1/3 of the paste of the beginning then to place above 2/3 of

the earpieces drained and rinsed of their syrup.
Make marbling on top with the preparation of the
cup. Then put the rest of the dough (the ears and
the chocolate aspect are hidden normally).
Dice the rest of the earlobes and scatter them visibly on top.
Bake in the oven at 185°C for 45 minutes.
The cake should come out golden with a well swollen
dome and visible apricot pieces. The tip of the knife
should come out dry if it is well baked.
Serve warm with a scoop of vanilla ice cream.

CHOCOLATE RICE CAKE

very easy

Ingredients

1 round glass of rice
1l whole milk
200g baking chocolate
4 tablespoons of sugar
1 packet of vanilla sugar
4 eggs

Preparation

Cook a glass of round rice in slightly salted water.
Boil the milk, chocolate, sugar, vanilla sugar and cooked rice.
Remove from the heat and add 4 whole eggs.
Cook for about 1/2 hour in the oven at medium heat (160°C).

CHOCOLATE YOGHURT CAKE WITH PASSOA

very easy

Ingredients

1 yurt
2 pots of flour (yoghurt pot)
1 jar of cornstarch
1 jar of sugar
1 jar of oil
3 eggs
1 sachet of yeast
1 sachet of vanilla sugar
Chocolate powder
2 passoa, to give a nice little taste (1)

Preparation

In your food processor, mix the yogurt, flour, cornstarch, sugars, oil and eggs. Add the yeast, and the chocolate (until the dough is dark enough). Then once everything is well mixed, without lumps, pour the passoa.
Pour the preparation into a well-oiled cake tin so that it doesn't stick and bake for about 30 minutes in a 180°C oven.
Enjoy your meal.
(1) [Note Marmiton - passoa: bright red liqueur, 20°, based on passion fruit juice].

YOGHURT CAKE, PEAR CHOCOLATE ALMOND

very easy

Ingredients

1 yurt
2 jars of sugar
1 pot of flour
2 jars of almond powder
3 eggs
1 sachet of baking powder
100g of chocolate
1 box of leeks in syrup

Preparation

Mix the yoghurt, sugar, flour, almond, yeast and eggs.
Dice the pears and add them to the mixture with the chocolate.
Cook for 30-40 minutes at 200°C.

YOGHURT, APPLE AND CHOCOLATE CAKE

easy

Ingredients

1 yurt
2 jars of sugar
2 tablespoons of olive oil
3 eggs
2.5 Flour jars
1/2 bag of yeast
1 sachet of vanilla sugar
2 apples
60g of dark chocolate
1 butternut for the mould

Preparation

Preheat the oven to 180°C (thermostat 6).
Generously butter a cake tin.
Peel the apples, remove the center and cut them into slices.
Using a paring knife, grate the chocolate into a bowl.
In a bowl, empty the yoghurt, add the two jars of sugar. Mix in.
Add the olive oil, stir well.
Separate the whites from the yolks, add the yolks to
the yoghurt-sugar mixture. Set aside the whites.
Add the flour, yeast and vanilla sugar to the preparation.
Whisk the whites until stiff and fold them
gently into the mixture.

Stir in the chocolate shavings.
Line the mould with a layer of apple slices.
Pour a layer of dough, cover with a layer of apple. Iterate until there is no more dough or apple.
Bake for about 45 minutes, check the baking time with the tip of a knife.

YOGHURT, COCONUT AND CHOCOLATE CAKE

very easy

Ingredients

1 natural yogurt
1 jar of yogurt) oil
2 jars of powdered sugar
3 pots of flour
3 eggs
1 sachet of baking powder
1 packet of grated coconut
1 teaspoon of liquid vanilla extract

Preparation

Preheat the oven to 180°C (thermostat 6).
Pour the yoghurt into a bowl. Use the pot as a measure.
Add the oil, sugar, flour, yeast, eggs, grated coconut and vanilla extract. Mix vigorously to obtain a homogeneous dough.
Butter a high rimmed non-stick pan and pour the mixture into it. Bake at 180°C for about 30 minutes.
When it is cooked, let it cool to room temperature and unmould it.
Finally prepare the chocolate icing by melting the chocolate with the butter in a saucepan. Once it is done, coat the top of the cake and let it cool.

You can decorate the cake with whipped cream which you arrange all around the cake just before serving.

YOGHURT CAKE WITH DARK CHOCOLATE 'CRUNCHY' LAYER

very easy

Ingredients

1 natural yogurt
2 jars of flour
2 jars of cornstarch
2 jars of caster sugar
1/2 jar of oil
7.5g vanilla sugar
3 eggs
11g of baking powder

Preparation

Mix all the ingredients for the yoghurt cake.
Place in a buttered, non-stick cake tin.
Bake for 15 minutes at 175°C, take it out and make
a slit 1 cm deep all the way through.
Put it back in the oven for 25-30 minutes. Check the
cooking with the point of a knife, it must come out.
Put the chocolate squares, sugar and liquid cream together
and melt not too liquid . (It's faster in the microwave!)
Unmould the cake after 1 hour of cooling, cut
it horizontally in the middle in two.
Spread with a knife the chocolate on 2 mm. Not thicker

than the thickness of a plate of chocolate because otherwise it will be too hard to crunch in the end. Don't spread too much at the edge either as in welding the two parts of the cake will settle down a bit.
Put in the fridge at least 1 hour before serving!

CINNAMON AND ORANGE CAKE (CHOCOLATE ICING)

very easy

Ingredients

1 natural yogurt
2 jars of sugar
3 pots of flour
3 eggs
1 jar of oil
1 untreated orange
4 teaspoons of cinnamon

Preparation

Pour the yoghurt into a container.
Add the sugar and the three egg yolks; set aside
the whites to whip them later.
Mix everything together and add the oil, then the flour.
It is advisable to put the oil before the flour so
that the preparation is easier to mix.
Add the cinnamon to the mixture.
Squeeze the juice of 1/2 orange, then zest the
peel and add it to the preparation.
Beat the egg whites until stiff and fold them into the mixture.
Pour into an oiled and floured mould and bake
at 180°C (Th 6) for about 35 min.

For the icing, melt the chocolate and butter in the microwave and spread over the cooled cake.

EASY CHOCOLATE NOUGATINE CAKE

very easy

Ingredients

1 natural yogurt
2 jars of powdered sugar
3 egg trails
3 pots of flour
1/2 bag of yeast
1/2 jar of oil
3 tablespoons of fresh cream
1/2 jar of coconut powder
90g of nougatine in bag
100g of dark chocolate in a bar

Preparation

Preheat your oven to 180°C.
In a salad bowl mix: the yoghurt, then the sugar, then the whole eggs, then the flour, then the yeast, then the oil, then the fresh cream, then the coconut.
Then add the nougatine but keep some to put on top of the preparation before cooking.
Coarsely grate the chocolate bar so that there are big and small pieces (I do it with a knife). Then add the chocolate to the preparation and, as for the nougatine, keep some for the top of the cake. Generously butter a mould, incorporate the preparation and sprinkle the rest of the nougatine and grated chocolate on

top (which will give a very crispy cake top, hummm...). Put in the oven at 180°C during 40 mn and check the cooking with a knife. Leave to cool for a few minutes and unmould. Slightly lukewarm or cold it's really a delight ! Bon appétit !

CHOCOLATE FILLED YOGHURT CAKE

very easy

Ingredients

1 natural yogurt
3 egg trails
1/2 jar of oil
1 jar of sugar
2 jars of flour
1 sachet of yeast
1 sachet of vanilla sugar

Preparation

Mix the sugar and the eggs until the mixture whitens. Add the flour and baking powder. Stir then add the yoghurt, oil and vanilla sugar. Pour the preparation into a buttered mould and bake for 20-30 minutes at 180°C. When the cake is baked, unmould it and let it cool down. In the meantime gently melt the chocolate with the butter and milk. Mix well.
Cut the cake in half and fill it with the chocolate mixture.

CHOCOLATE, HONEY, RUM SOFT CAKE

easy

Ingredients

1 natural yogurt
70s sugar
80g of flour
50g of chocolate
1 tablespoon of rum
20g of butter
3 eggs
2 tablespoons of honey
2 tablespoons of neutral oil

Preparation

In a salad bowl, mix the plain yogurt, sugar, flour and eggs. Melt the butter with the chocolate over a low heat. As soon as the mixture is homogeneous pour into the preparation. Add the honey and the rum. Pour into a buttered mould and cook for 35 minutes at 180°C (thermostat 6). Let cool and enjoy.

WALNUT CAKE AND SIMPLE CHOCOLATE ICING

very easy

Ingredients

1 natural yogurt (100 g)
yoghurt pot can be used as a measuring cup.
2 jars of flour (200 g)
1 jar of sugar (100 g)
1/2 jar of oil (7 cl)
3 eggs
1/2 bag of yeast
1 sachet of vanilla sugar
100g of powdered walnuts according to taste

Preparation

Preheat the oven to 180°C, thermostat 6.
In a salad bowl, mix the plain yoghurt, eggs, sugar, oil, yeast, powdered nuts and finally the flour.
Mix everything well and pour into a mould.
Put in the oven for 30 min.
Once the cake has cooled, prepare the icing by melting the chocolate in a small saucepan over a low heat and then add the liquid cream.
Spread the icing with a brush on the cake and decorate with walnut kernels.

Set aside in a cool place for the icing to harden.

CHOCOLATE HAZELNUT YOGHURT AND CHESTNUT FLOUR CAKE

very easy

Ingredients

1 yurt nature (even a 0%), the pot is used as a measure
1 pot of flour
1 pot of chestnut flour
1 pot of hazelnut powder
3/4 jar of sugar (preferably brown)
1/2 jar of melted butter
3 eggs
1 sachet of yeast
1 pinch of baking soda (optional)
2 teaspoons of sweetened cocoa powder
30g of chocolate (or coarsely crushed pastry chocolate)
1 pinch of salt

Preparation

Preheat the oven to 180°C (thermostat 6).
Mix together the two sifted flours, hazelnut powder, sugar, yeast and bicarbonate.
Make a well in the center of the mixture and add the

melted butter, the eggs and the yoghurt.
Separate the dough obtained into two equal parts. Add the cocoa and the nuggets in one part and leave the other part untouched.
Butter a small cake mould (or a missed one) unless you use a silicone mould.
And pour alternately plain dough then chocolate dough until exhausted.
Then place in the preheated oven and bake for 35 minutes.
Leave to cool and then unmould the cake and enjoy!

YOGHURT, MINT AND CHOCOLATE CAKE

easy

Ingredients

1 0% natural yoghurt in a jar
1/2 jar of cornstarch
1 pot of almond powder
1 pot of flour
1/4 jar of fructose (resistant to cooking
or 1 jar of powdered sugar)
1 sachet of yeast
1 jar of mint syrup (without sugar)
1 pinch of salt
3 eggs
1 pot of chocolate

Preparation

Preheat the oven to 180°C (thermostat 6).
Mix all the powders and add the yoghurt. Mix all the powders and add the yoghurt.
Add the mint. Mix all powders.
Add eggs and chocolate chips.
Put everything in a cake dish and let it cook at 180°C (thermostat 6) for 40 minutes.

YOGHURT, BANANA AND CHOCOLATE CAKE

very easy

Ingredients

1 natural yogurt and its pot
3/4 jar of yoghurt oil vacuum
2 eggs
2 jars of sugar
1 sachet of vanilla sugar
3 pots of flour
1 sachet of yeast
3 ripe bananas
100g of dark chocolate

Preparation

Preheat your oven.
Put all ingredients in a container as you go.
Mix until the dough becomes fluid (without too many lumps).
Cut your bananas into slices, chop the chocolate into chips and add to the mixture.
Bake at 150°C (gas mark 5) for about 40-45 minutes (until the top is golden brown).

YOGHURT CAKE, WHITE CHOCOLATE AND SPECULOOS TOPPING

easy

Ingredients

1 natural or sweet yogurt
2 jars of flour
1 packet of yeast
3/4 jar of oil
1 jar of brown sugar
3 eggs

Preparation

For the yoghurt cake:
Preheat the oven to 200°C.
Mix all ingredients together in order.
Put the mixture in a springform pan and bake at 200°C for about 45 min.
In the meantime make the topping:
Whip the fresh cream with a mixer.
Grate the white chocolate and melt it in a bain marie until smooth melted chocolate is obtained.
Remove the pan from the heat and add the cream.

Mix the speculoos cookies.
When the cake is cooked, coat it with the white chocolate-cream mixture and then cover it with the mixed speculoos.

YOGHURT, CHOCOLATE, CINNAMON AND RUM CAKE

very easy

Ingredients

1 yurt (bifidus for me) which will be used as a measure
3 eggs
1 jar of cane sugar 1 sachet of vanilla sugar
1/2 jar of oil (sunflower for example)
1 jar of cornstarch
2 pots of flour T45
1 sachet of baking powder
2 rhum
1 teaspoon of cinnamon
200g of pastry chocolate

Preparation

Mix the yoghurt and egg yolks. Then add sugars and cinnamon.
Add the oil.
Add the cornstarch, flour and yeast.
Add 2 corks of rum.
Melt the chocolate by putting it 1 min in
the microwave at full power.

Beat the egg whites until stiff and fold them into the dough.
Arrange the dough in a cake tin.
Cook for 10 min at 180°C (thermostat 6) then
35 min at 150°C (thermostat 5).
Enjoy your meal ;-)

VERY QUICK YOGHURT AND CHOCOLATE CAKE

very easy

Ingredients

1 yurt (whose pot is then used as a dosing device)
2 jars of flour
1 jar of sugar
3/4 jar of oil
3 eggs
1 sachet of yeast
200g of chocolate for pastry

Preparation

Preheat the oven to 180°C (thermostat 6) and melt the chocolate (without butter or anything else).
In the meantime, mix all the other ingredients (mixing first the baking powder and flour, otherwise they mix badly).
Add the melted chocolate.
Butter a baking tin and pour the dough.
Put in the oven for 15 min at 180°C (gas mark 6), then 15 min at 150°C (gas mark 5).
Check the baking: it must be baked on top and moist inside.

RASPBERRY YOGHURT AND CHOCOLATE CAKE

very easy

Ingredients

1 raspberry yogurt
3 pots of yoghurt) of flour
1 jar of cornstarch
2 jars of sugar
3/4 jar of oil
3 eggs
1 sachet of baking powder
2 tablespoons of cocoa (chocolate powder)

Preparation
Mix the ingredients one by one. Put in the oven for 3/4 of an hour. Thermostat :5 or 190°.

GERMAN RED WINE, CHOCOLATE AND CINNAMON CAKE (ROTWEINKUCHEN)

very easy

Ingredients

200g of butter
120g of sugar
1 sachet of vanilla sugar
5 eggs
25cl of red wine
100g dark chocolate grated or in chips
1 teaspoon of cinnamon to taste
10g of cocoa
200g of hazelnut pieces
150g of flour
1 sachet of baking powder

Preparation

Preheat the oven to 180°C (thermostat 6).
Whip the butter with the sugars and the eggs in a salad bowl.
Pour in the red wine and the chocolate then stir
well. Add the cinnamon and cocoa.
Quickly toast the hazelnuts in the frying pan, let them

cool down, then mix them with the flour and the baking powder. Add this mixture to the dough.
Bake for about 45 minutes, less (35 minutes) if you want a melt-in-the-mouth cake (personally that's how I prefer it!) and 60 minutes if you want it well baked.
Serve with a scoop of vanilla ice cream or heavy cream, or slices of apples browned in butter.

TIBUR'S CAKE (SOFT PEANUT-CHOCOLATE)

easy

Ingredients

200g of butter
150g of sugar
4 eggs (white and yellow separated)
150g salted peanuts
100g of flour
150g of chocolate
1 teaspoon of salt
1 teaspoon of vanilla flavouring

Preparation

Mix the butter ointment (softened in the microwave) with the sugar. Add the egg yolks.
Chop the peanuts as finely as possible (with an electric chopper, for example) and add them to the dough. Stir well. Add the flour.
Whisk the egg whites until stiff with the salt. Stir in gently. Add the chocolate chips.
Pour in a round buttered mould and put in the oven at thermostat 6 (180°C) for about 30 minutes: a knife blade must come out dry.

DANISH CHOCOLATE CAKE

very easy

Ingredients

200g of butter
180g of sugar
1 tablespoon of honey
1 packet of vanilla sugar
150g of chopped almonds
200g dark chocolate, chopped
100g of flour
5 eggs
1 teaspoon baking powder
1 tablespoon of rum

Preparation

Preheat your oven to 180°C.
In a saucepan, put the butter, sugar and vanilla sugar.
Melt over very low heat until the sugar melts.
Then add the almonds, chocolate and honey, and a little bit
of rum, continuing to stir until the chocolate is melted.
Remove the pan from the heat and stir the mixture to cool.
Meanwhile, separate the yolks from the whites. Mix the flour
with the baking powder. Whisk the egg whites until stiff.
When your mixture has cooled, add the egg yolks
and mix. Then put flour and baking powder, mix.
And finally, beat the egg whites until stiff.

Pour the whole in a buttered and floured mould (except tart mould) and put in the oven, the first half hour on 180 degrees and another 1 hour on 150°C.
Make a chocolate topping and coat the cake.

CHOCOLATE FONDANT WITH THE HEART OF JAM

easy

Ingredients

200g of butter
200g of chocolate
100g of flour
150g of sugar
3 eggs
1 jar of jam of your choice

Preparation

Preheat the oven to 200°C (thermostat 6-7).
Melt the butter and chocolate in a bain-marie. (Stir from time to time).
Meanwhile, in a salad bowl mix the flour, sugar and eggs.
When the butter and the chocolate are melted, incorporate them into the preparation. To mix.
Pour half of the final preparation in a buttered cake mould.
Put in the oven for 10 min maximum.
Then take the cake out of the oven and spread with jam (I like it very much with Orange-Clementine jam).
Pour over the other half of the preparation.
Bake again 10 min or more depending if you like melting or very melting for the gourmands !!

EXTRA SOFT CHOCOLATE-ALMOND-ORANGE BLOSSOM MUFFINS

easy

Ingredients

200g of butter
200g of chocolate
150g of sugar
150g almond powder
100g of flour
4 eggs
1 yurt
2 sachets of vanilla sugar
1 sachet of yeast
1 tablespoon orange blossom water

Preparation

Preheat the oven to 170°C (thermostat 5-6).
Melt the chocolate and butter in a bain-marie.
In a salad bowl, mix the flour and baking powder.
Add almond powder, eggs, yoghurt and orange blossom.
Incorporate the sugars then mix quickly
with the chocolate preparation.

Mix everything together and pour into muffin tins.
Bake for 30 minutes.

CHOCOLATE CAKE

easy

Ingredients

200g of butter
200g of dark chocolate
200g of powdered sugar
5 eggs
40g of flour
Butter for the mould

Preparation

Preheat the oven to 190°C (th.6-)
Cut the butter and chocolate into pieces and melt them in the microwave or in a bain-marie.
Whisk the preparation and add the powdered sugar.
Incorporate the eggs one by one, mixing well, then add the flour.
Butter the mould and pour the preparation into it.
Make copper during 25 minutes for a soft cooking in heart or during 30 minutes for a firmer consistency.

CHOCOLATE-ORANGE BROWNIES

very easy

Ingredients

200g of butter
200g noir dessert chocolate
200g caster sugar
4 eggs
100g of flour
1 teaspoon of orange
20cl of orange juice

Preparation

Preheat the oven to 150°C (thermostat 5).
Melt the chocolate, broken in a saucepan, in a bain-marie, then add the butter cut into pieces and mix carefully to obtain a creamy sauce.
Let cool a few minutes.
In a salad bowl, whip the whole eggs, incorporate the sugar and mix until the mixture whitens.
Add the orange extract and the juice. Then stir in the chocolate sauce.
Then pour in the flour, mixing vigorously to avoid lumps.
Pour the dough into a square or rectangular pan.
Bake for 20 to 25 minutes and then cut the brownie into small squares of 5 cm side.

MOELLEUX CHOCOLAT

easy

Ingredients

200g of butter
200g of pastry chocolate
200g of sugar
25cl of liquid cream
4 eggs
5 tablespoons of flour

Preparation

This is very fast if you have a microwave…
Melt the butter, chocolate and liquid cream in a large bowl. Mix well after… (attention: the preparation must remain lukewarm after the exit of the microwaves)
Add sugar, flour and whole eggs (beaten beforehand to incorporate more easily).
Pour the preparation into a preferably disposable aluminium mould (for a better heat distribution, unless you are cooking it in the microwave as you should not put an aluminium mould in the microwave).
Cooking time: 15 minutes at 180°C (thermostat 6).
When taken out of the oven, the softness should be 'barely cooked' in the center of the mould.
Leave to cool and then put in the fridge, which will harden the center just cooked.
For the chef's tip, you can add a few drops of vanilla extract or bitter orange.

An advice to taste your softness: to pass it 15 seconds maximum power in the microwave. It will come out melting at heart...
It is magic!
Bon appétit.

IMPRINT

All rights reserved

Mindful Publishing
We help you to publish your book!
By

TTENTION Inc.
Wilmington - DE19806
Trolley Square 20c

All rights reserved

Instagram: mindful_publishing
Contact: mindful.publishing@web.de
Contact2: mindful.publishing@protonmail.com

Printed in Great Britain
by Amazon